MAKING A GOOD LIFE BETTER

SYLVESTER HENRY III

© 2014 SYLVESTER HENRY. ALL RIGHTS RESERVED

ALL RIGHTS RESERVED. NO PART OF THIS WORK MAY BE REPRODUCED OR STORED IN AN INFORMATIONAL RETRIEVAL SYSTEM, WITHOUT THE EXPRESS PERMISSION OF THE PUBLISHER IN WRITING.

ISBN:0692295267

PUBLISHED BY:
10-10-10 PUBLISHING
MARKHAM, ON
CANADA

Contents

Foreword	1
Acres of Diamonds	3
Chapter 1: Desire	5
Chapter 2: Visualization	9
Chapter 3: Affirmations	15
Chapter 4: Be Grateful	19
Chapter 5: Expect Prosperity	25
Chapter 6: Self-Talk	29
Chapter 7: Health (Your First Wealth)	35
Chapter 8: Loving Relationships	39
Chapter 9: Stay Positive	43
Chapter 10: Put Your New Power to Work!	47

I would like to thank my beautiful wife
Antonette Toney Henry for her love and support.
This book would not have been possible without her.
Together we are Making A Good Life Better.
I love my Suga!

Foreword

Making a Good Life Better is a powerful book that will help you to attain the desires and dreams you have for yourself. Sylvester has really put together a dynamic 10-step process that will help you to improve in all areas of your life. *Making a Good Life Better* teaches you how to get your desires met, using techniques that will launch you into prosperity. This book teaches you the power of your thoughts and how very important your thoughts are in creating the life you desire. *Making a Good Life Better* teaches you how vitally important your self-talk is. You go throughout your day talking to yourself, not even conscious of what you are saying, to yourself or about yourself. This book will help you to become aware of your self-talk. *Making a Good Life Better* was written in the hope that these 10 steps will help you get all the desires of your heart. If you desire health this book will help you, if you desire more money this book will help you, if you desire a loving relationship this book will help you. *Making a Good Life Better* emphasizes that what you visualize for yourself and feel will ultimately come true in physical form. I know you will find a wealth of encouraging information in this first edition of *Making a Good Life Better*!

Raymond Aaron
New York Times Bestselling Author

Acres of Diamonds

The story was about a farmer who lived in Africa and, through a visitor, became tremendously excited about looking for diamonds. Diamonds were already discovered in abundance on the African continent, and this farmer got so excited about the idea of millions of dollars' worth of diamonds that he sold his farm to head out to the diamond line. He wandered all over the continent, as the years slipped by, constantly searching for diamonds and wealth, which he never found. Eventually he went completely broke and threw himself into a river and drowned. Meanwhile, the new owner of his farm picked up an unusual looking rock about the size of a country egg and put it on his mantle as a sort of curiosity. A visitor stopped by and in viewing the rock practically went into terminal convulsions. He told the new owner of the farm that the funny looking rock on his mantle was about the biggest diamond that had ever been found. The new owner of the farm said, "Heck, the whole farm is covered with them" -- and sure enough it was. The farm turned out to be the Kimberly Diamond Mine...the richest the world has ever known. The original farmer was literally standing on "Acres of Diamonds" until he sold his farm.

Dr. Conwell learned from the story of the farmer and continued to teach its moral. Each of us is right in the middle of our own

"Acre of Diamonds", if only we would realize it and develop the ground we are standing on before charging off in search of greener pastures.

Dr. Conwell told this story many times and attracted enormous audiences. He told the story long enough to have raised the money to start the college for underprivileged deserving students. When Dr. Russell H. Conwell talked about each of us being right on our own "Acre of Diamonds", he meant it. This story does not get old...it will be true forever...

Chapter 1
Desire

The power to be and have what we want is found within us. Everything we desire and wish to materialize in our lives we can have. We need a true desire for what we want in order to get it. In this first chapter we will talk about desire.

Desire, according to Webster, is a strong feeling of wanting something. To crave, to want, to long for something.

This chapter will teach you how to obtain all that you desire. The tools that you need to obtain your desires are already within you. The desires you have are already manifested right now in your life. What you want already exists now in your life. You know that there is so much more you are capable of than what you are doing right now. The feeling you have in your inner spirit tells you that you can and will be more than you are right now. One of your goals in making a good life better is to take hold of your desires now. Know that what you desire is what you deserve. If you can think of your desire you can surely have it. All the things that you desire must first be present in your mind. It's up to you to participate in the world that you have created in your mind hold to that desire.

As stated earlier, desire is a strong feeling of wanting something, to crave, to long for something. That is exactly the feeling you need in order to get what you desire out of life. You need to crave, to long for health, wealth, abundance and loving relationships, Whatever you desire is what you will have. You need to be passionate about your desire in order to bring it into your life. It is our nature to want to become all we can be; we can't help it. Once you have that longing for something it will lead you to some sort of action to take. It will be an action that will just come to you seemingly "out of the blue". Once you have that clear mental image of what you want, it will come to you. Maybe you want a healthier body, keeping that desire in mind will bring an action for you to take. Your desire for a healthy body may lead you to eating healthier or exercising more. Okay, so you don't like to exercise. Eventually your desire will push away that thought of not liking to exercise because you know a part of having a healthy body is exercising.

If it is financial peace you desire, a way to obtain that financial peace will make its way to you. Set your mind on the desired amount you want to have, and have that craving -- that strong feeling of wanting. A way will surely be made clear to you. Here is a personal example. My desire is to make my yearly income my monthly income. I desired that specific amount and ways are being shown to me now in the present. I held that desire close and ways of making it happen began to show up.

Writing down your desires reinforces the desire even more.

Write down your desires and review them often. Keep copies in your wallet, in your purse, on the mirror in the bathroom. After a while you will not have to read them. They will become part of you, and you will find yourself thinking of your desires all the time. And before you even realize it all your desires will have been met.

Stay focused and your desires will find you. Things will begin to happen for you. Doors will start to open for you. People will want to help you in obtaining your desires.

A quick story on how I began my journey on prosperity... I was working a regular nine-to-five job, not very happy, and like you I knew that I deserved better for myself than what I was giving myself. My car was being smog checked. In the smog shop was a Success magazine. I had never seen or heard of Success magazine. It piqued my interest and I picked it up. I opened it up to an article by the great Jim Rohn. At the time, I had never heard of Jim Rohn; however, as I write this book I am very familiar with him. Jim Rohn is considered by most in the business world as the authority in business philosophy. He told his story of being a farm boy raised in obscurity, and how he rose to success. I read his story and knew if Jim could make his desires come true so could I ... and so can you.

Sylvester Henry

Hold your desires close to you. Always keep in the front of your mind exactly want you want. A thought that is continually being played in your mind will become a thing in your life. Always keep your mind on the thing you desire. What you do not desire needs no attention from you!

Be sure to check out the four free bonuses I have for you at www.makingagoodlifebetter.com

Chapter 2
Visualization

The dictionary defines visualization as the formation of mental visual images or pictures. Images and pictures that are actually seen in the eyes of the mind. We all visualize, whether we realize it or not. Most likely you are visualizing right now as you are reading this. In the morning as you are preparing for your day you are visualizing. We form mental pictures as we start our day; some good some not so good.

When you get up in the morning your new thoughts will be of only the things you want to experience. You will learn to "create your day" in the manner in which you want it to go instead of allowing your mind to just drift from thought to thought. You will begin to direct your day through visualizing it on purpose. When you get up in the morning visualize your day, see it in the eyes of your mind. For example, say to yourself "I am grateful to be able to take part in this today. I will have a pleasant drive to work. I will have an awesome day interacting with my coworkers. I will keep a positive attitude even when things may be contrary. The meeting I am holding will captivate and impress everyone in attendance. God is in control and all things go my way". Visualize it and see the changes you want take place. The bible says in Romans 4:17 "Calleth those things which be not as though they were". That's exactly what you will learn to do.

Visualize it as if you already have the desires of your heart. Visualize the loving relationship as if you are already in a loving relationship with your prince charming or the queen of your dreams. Visualize your health as only excellent and vibrant. Visualize as if you are free from debt, free from all monetary obligations. See yourself living in abundance. When I use the word "see" I am not meaning seeing with your physical eye. I am speaking of the eyes in your mind, the eyes that are located in your imagination. This is where visualization is done; this is where all the seeds are planted. Whatever you can picture in your mind, you have the power to bring it into your life.

Make the visualization a grand picture. Make it huge. You are not limited by money; these are your dreams and desires. See it in your mind's eye just as you want to experience it. Do not be afraid to make the picture larger than your wildest dreams; you deserve as much. Get greedy, get beside yourself. Visualize the health you deserve, travel, mansions -- yes mansions with an s if that's what you want. Use the gift of your imagination to create the life you want.

You have probably heard of the phrase "what you see is what you get". I have heard that almost all my life but it never hit me until I started to practice visualization. What a gift it is! It is such a powerful and truthful statement, "what you see is what you get". What you see in the eyes of your mind is what you get and what you become. It may sound a little over-simplified but it is true. "What you see is what you get"! The technique of visualization is very powerful. You cannot receive anything unless you can conceive it in the eyes of your mind. You must visualize it first and believe you can and will have it. All you have to do is determine clearly and decisively exactly what you want.

If you want to be healthy you have to get a picture of yourself being healthy in the eyes of your mind. You may write down "I want to be a healthy fit 120 pounds and wear my high school prom dress." See yourself healthy and lean. See yourself in the prom dress. If you are a guy picture yourself at your ideal weight looking fit in your new business suit. Maybe you want to earn more money. Be specific as to the amount of money you want to earn. If it's an extra ten thousand dollars a month, visualize yourself earning exactly that. Visualize what you will do with the extra money. When visualizing make sure you acknowledge the feeling that you will have as you are visualizing. There will be a feeling of excitement, expectancy, pride and richness. Enjoy that feeling as you are visualizing what you want to experience in your life. Really put yourself in the environment you want to create for yourself.

To aid in your visualization I recommend that you create a vision board. You may have heard of this technique before. A vision board is a poster board on which you will put all the pictures of the things you desire in your life. If you want a beautiful home on the beach, find a picture in a magazine of a beautiful home on the beach, cut it out and put it on your vision board. If you want a fit body, find a picture with the same body you desire, cut it out put it on your vision board. Cut out the face and add a picture of your face on the body. That way you can see exactly what you will look like when you reach your ideal weight. Put the amount of money you want to earn on your vision board. Whatever it takes to get the feeling of what you want is what we are shooting for.

The vision board is a powerful tool that will allow you to see your future successes. You are literally creating your own reality.

You should put your vision board in a place where you will see it first thing in the morning and before you go to bed at night. This will help to seed your subconscious mind. Recall what you want as a memory of something that really happened. When you visualize in this manner you can make your subconscious believe that it actually happened. I don't have the expertise to explain the workings of the subconscious mind but you can visit www.makingagoodlifebetter.com and I will recommend some wonderful references. I also have a picture of my vision board posted there for you to see.

You will soon find out that, as the images in your life start to change, your life will begin to change to fit those mental pictures. You will find that people and other resources will seem to show up at the right time to help you bring those mental thoughts into realities. I have my vision board on the wall in my bedroom. I see it first thing in the morning as I get up, and it's the last thing I look at before I go to bed. Looking at your vision board and feeling each experience of each picture will put you on the road to what you are visualizing.

Be sure to go to www.makingagoodlifebetter.com and get the four bonuses I have for you!

Chapter 3
Affirmations

Webster's dictionary defines affirmation as an act of affirming: to declare positively something to be true. An affirmation is a strong statement from your conscious mind to your subconscious mind. It is a statement that you want to declare for your life. It could be an affirmation of health. It could be an affirmation of wealth. It could be an affirmation of a loving nourishing relationship. Whatever you want for your life you can affirm in a statement of your own choosing. These positive statements will help drive out old negative thoughts you have been accepting as true in your life. The affirmation should have "I" in it. The "I" will make it personal to you. I am… and then the positive affirmation. As an example, if you are not in the physical shape you would like to be in, an affirmation could be "I am improving on my physical condition one day at a time". This is a positive statement and it uses a present tense. If you use this affirmation, repeat it as often as you can. Make it a habit to say to yourself "I am in great physical shape" or "I am improving on my physical condition one day at a time". You will soon find yourself watching what you eat, you will begin exercising, you will find yourself subscribing to health magazines. You may even find yourself instructing a yoga class.

Affirmations can help to bring all your possibilities to life. When you state your affirmation make sure you state it with a lot of emotion. Put a lot of feeling earnest behind the affirmation. Feel the confidence, the self-esteem boost of being what you want to be or become. If it's financial freedom you want feel the feeling that would come with financial freedom and abundance. Do not be afraid to dream big.

One of my favorite affirmations is "I am grateful to be healthy, wealthy and wise". That affirmation declares all the things I desire to be. It is personal and positive. It runs through my mind countless times a day. It boosts my self-esteem, and gives me confidence as I go about my day-to-day business. I affirm as if it is a current fact in my life, as if the thing already exists in my life. This is one of the great things about our subconscious mind. It activates on the present, the now. I am, I earn, I live or I love. When you use present tense, your subconscious will direct you to the changes you need to make in order for your desires to become the reality you want to live. I have a friend that speaks affirmations over his life all the time. Every time we get together I hear the affirmation over and over again. I can actually see his affirmation taking place and being a part of his life. Every word my friend speaks is an actual part of his life. The affirmations so often consist of "I am too old", "I feel bad", " I can't do that", "I don't have any money". Those affirmations are being accepted by his subconscious mind as being true. My friend is speaking all those negative things into reality.

We can easily get caught up in the news of the day and began speaking of all the problems of the world. The world's problems are not your problem. You have to affirm how you want your day to go, every single day.

We have help from our subconscious mind. Our subconscious mind takes whatever we present to it as true. So always present to it only what you want to experience through your affirmations. Once your subconscious accepts your affirmation as true, it will lead you to do things that you would only do if indeed your affirmation were true.

Speak your affirmation over and over again with intensity so it becomes a part of you. Learn to call the affirmation up without even thinking about it. You will begin to call it up subconsciously because of the repetition of the affirmation.

I guess I can explain the power of affirmations like this. Your mind is like a magnet. You can draw things to yourself. Repetition of your affirmation will begin to draw the things you want into your life, and you will be amazed at how your life will began to change. Be sure to go to www.makinga goodlifebetter.com and post your favorite affirmation. Also check out the four free bonuses I have for you!

Chapter 4
Be Grateful

Being grateful is one of the most powerful conditions you can allow yourself to be in. Being grateful for what you have now will bring even more things into your life to be grateful for. Be grateful for the job you have right now. Be grateful for the neighborhood you live in, be grateful for the car that you have, be grateful for the relationships that you are in. You have to be grateful for what you have in order to get the things that you truly desire in life. What you have in your life right now is a blessing and you should be grateful for it. You may be earning $100,000 a year, you may be earning $50,000. Whatever it is, be grateful for it. Maybe you have a goal to live in a beautiful 4,000 sq. ft. home in South Florida. In order to help bring that into realty you must be grateful for the home you live in now. Look around your home or your apartment and be grateful for the furniture you have. Be grateful for the dishes you have, be grateful for the windows that you are able to look out of and enjoy the beautiful sunshine. Be grateful for the conditions in which you live because in fact you created those conditions. Be grateful knowing that you will get exactly what you desire by being grateful for what you have.

You must be grateful for the things you have been gifted with so far. If your health is not where you would like it to be right now, speak loudly in gratitude for the health that you do have. Years ago I purchased a pickup truck from a coworker. When I first saw the truck I thought to myself what a nice looking truck. Later that night I was speaking with this coworker, not knowing then that the truck belonged to him. As we were speaking, he mentioned that he was in the market for a new truck and wanted to sell his current truck. I asked what kind of truck he had. He named the model and sure enough it was the same truck that I had been admiring in the parking lot. I asked him how much he wanted to sell it for, he named the price and two days later I owned the truck. As the years have gone by the excitement has worn off a bit. However, that truck has served me well. As the truck got older, more repairs than just general maintenance needed to be done. Radiator, heater, core fuel pump and catalytic converter all needed repair or replacement in the last couple years. Looking back I realized it is just things that a 13-year-old truck would need at some point or another. But at the time I was fed up with all the repairs it needed, and I wanted another truck "now". I had forgotten how grateful I was when I first purchased the truck. I found myself calling my truck a piece of junk saying things like "I'm tired of throwing money at it" or "I'm going to sell this piece of crap as soon as I can." Instead of being grateful for my truck and being grateful for the fact that I could pay for the repairs, saying things like that was stopping the flow of more things to be grateful for. I soon realized that my thoughts towards my truck were not in line with gratitude. So I started to be grateful for being able to get it repaired when it needed repairs. I was grateful that it got me back and forth throughout my day.

As I began to be grateful for my current truck, doors soon opened for me to get the truck I really wanted. Just a side note to the guys reading this book. Every man needs a truck! Although I have read recently in Texas there are more women purchasing trucks than men today. Anyway I digress.

I have found it doesn't matter who you are; being grateful seems to eliminate any negative conditions. The more things you are grateful for, the more things will be attracted into your life. Be grateful and you will start to see things that you haven't seen before. Things like having favor at the grocery store. You may have a few items and the person in front of you has a cart full and the person will let you go ahead of them. Be grateful for the favor you have in the parking lot, be grateful for the fact that you are always on time for work, be grateful for traffic, be grateful for the fact that your kids are doing their homework. Being grateful for whatever condition you find yourself in will bring more things into your life to be grateful for.

You may want to declare, I am grateful and I am so proud that I am currently earning the money that I need so that my wife is able to stay at home and take care of the children. Even if it has not yet manifested be grateful for it. The beautiful home, that awesome career, that invention, that book you want to write ... being grateful for it now will actually help propel it into existence. You are sending out a powerful signal that will not return void. Make a habit of speaking and thinking the things you are grateful for even though you can't see them yet. Say things like "I am awesome inventor", "I am an awesome husband", "I am an awesome wife and mother".

There is one other thing you should do, and that is to expect. Expect it! Always expect good things and you will receive good things into your life.

I have developed a habit of getting up in the morning and immediately thanking God for waking me up. Grateful that He allowed me to see another day. Grateful for the countless blessings that had to have taken place just to keep me throughout the night.

Go to www.makingagoodlifebetter.com there you will find a bonus chapter on the law of attraction. The law of attraction is really what we are putting to use when we are being grateful for what we have. We are using this law all the time whether we

Making a Good Life Better

know it or not. So let's use it with the intension of making a good life better.

Chapter 5
Expect Prosperity

Prosperity is the state of flourishing, thriving, having good fortune and/or successful social status. That definition seems pretty awesome to me. To flourish means to grow well. What an awesome opportunity you have to grow well. We all have a right to flourish and thrive, just as the definition states. Jesus said "I came that they might have life, and have it more abundantly." John 10:10. You have the God-given power to produce prosperity in all areas of your life. In your quest of making a good life better, you must develop a prosperity consciousness. Hold on to the thoughts you want to experience. One of the most important aspects of prosperity is nurturing and developing a prosperous mindset. Know that you are prosperous, and you will become more prosperous if that's what you really want. You deserve to live in abundance. You deserve to live a rich full life. Do not be ashamed by wanting to be prosperous. When you speak of prosperity around some of your associates they may think you are money hungry or greedy. Let them think whatever they want to think. Soon they will witness your success and will begin to ask what you are doing to be so prosperous. We all may want to be prosperous, but some believe it's not good to say it out loud around other people. That's really funny because we all want the same thing. Prosperity consciousness comes from thinking in the right way. By thinking success you will create success. The same goes for failure. If you think lack and failure that's what you will get. "As a man thinketh within his heart so is he", the bible says. So it is true, to be prosperous we should speak of prosperity in our life. James Allen the philosopher puts it this way: "Man holds the key to every situation and contains within himself that transforming and regenerative agency by which he may make himself what he wills." So your wealth, health and happiness are within you!

That's exciting news for all of us. Our success is already within us; we just have to be aware of it. Your success and prosperity will be created mentally first. I am reminded of a good childhood friend of mine who began to work in a tire shop in high school. While most of us were making plans of college and military service, he was perfectly happy working at the tire shop. We all went our separate ways just as we had envisioned. At the 10-year high school reunion I learned that my friend was still in the tire shop. However, one thing was different. He owned the shop. As a matter of fact, he owned several tire shops throughout the city. He had a vision of what he wanted and he got exactly what he expected.

If you want health, develop a health consciousness. If you want wealth, develop a wealth consciousness. If you want prosperity, develop a prosperity consciousness. Believe you live in prosperity and you will begin to prosper. Say the words "I live in prosperity", "I live in prosperity", over and over again. Your words have power, the power to change your life, your circumstances, and your environment. The technique of repeating that small phrase makes it yours and limitless. Your words are the thoughts that you are and thoughts are creative. Creating your reality is as simple as just believing that there is only prosperity and that is the state in which you choose to live. Let's concentrate on financial prosperity here for a moment.

Money. Let's face it, in order to live, flourish and thrive in good fortune we must have money. In order to live like we want and to do and go where we want we need money. In my opinion we need lots of it. Do not be ashamed in wanting money. Wanting money is wanting health, loving relationships and great communities. Lack of money is poverty. Some may think of poverty as a virtue. Some people are actually taught this in churches. Poverty is not a virtue; it is a vice. If you have been living in lack or limitation you have been living in a vice. You are making a good life better by your new prosperous thinking. If you want money be specific as to the exact amount. If you want 500,000 dollars a year set your mind on 500,000 dollars a year. Think of that amount all the time. Have a picture of what 500,000 dollars look like. Get a feeling of 500,000 dollars a year. Start looking into what types of investments you would be interested in. Shop on the internet for things that a 500,000 dollar a year income could buy. You will soon start to develop the mindset of a millionaire. Get the feeling of success and prosperity. You will be led to a 500,000 dollar idea.

Hold the image of prosperity in the eyes of your mind and keep it there. Doors will begin to open for you that you could have only imagined.

Go to www.makingagoodlifebetter.com and check out the four bonuses. Also get your Making A Good Life Better T-shirt!

Deuteronomy 8:18
You shall remember the Lord your God, for it is he who gives you power to get wealth, that he may confirm his covenant that he swore to your fathers, as it is this day.

Chapter 6
Self-Talk

Each of us has an internal dialogue. We are in conversation with ourselves every minute of every day. We talk more to ourselves than to anyone else. What are the things we are saying to ourselves? What are we saying the most? Are they positive? Are they thoughts that will empower us? Does your self-talk consist of thoughts of what you want? Or is it thoughts of what you don't want? Saying things like "I'm too old", "I'm not smart enough to start a business", "I don't have what it takes", "he can do it but I can't". That kind of self-talk keeps millions of people from reaching their goals. We talk to ourselves subconsciously; we don't even think about it. We are constantly talking to ourselves all day long. Most of the time we do not realize that the self-talk is negative. All through the day destructive messages are allowed to penetrate our minds. You may see someone who is successful, someone who is making a good life better, and that inner voice tells you that "I can't do that, I'm not as smart as that person, I'm not as talented as he or she is." It may be you see someone who is in good physical shape, somebody who looks healthy, fit and good-looking, and you tell yourself "I can't be that disciplined to go to the gym. I'll never look that good."

I have found that oftentimes this form of thinking comes from the way we were brought up as children. The people who should have been nurturing us and telling us how great we are, and that we are creators who can be whatever we want to be, did just the opposite. Now some of those negative thoughts have taken root and are continuing to grow.

We can, however, reprogram ourselves. Start thinking about what's right with you instead of what's wrong with you. Stop rehearsing your mistakes and meditating on them. Remind yourself of what you can do. It doesn't matter how many times you've tried, it doesn't matter how many times you've failed. Tell yourself you are more than capable and pick yourself up and dust yourself off. Remind yourself that you are a leader, you are talented, you have what it takes. You can do whatever you want to do, only believe that you can. Our internal dialogue should always be positive and cheerful. We should always talk to ourselves with empowering affirmation. We have to get out of the habit of thinking negative thoughts about ourselves. Do not ever say "I can't do that." Get those negative phrases out of your vocabulary. If you make the mistake of dwelling on the negative things, surely the negative is what you will get. You may suffer some setbacks, you may have been treated unfairly, but don't allow that to pull you down by constantly thinking about it. Tell yourself "I was mistreated; I recognize that. However, I can't control that and I choose to move on." You must pay attention to your self-talk. Tell yourself "I have what it takes; I am empowered, I am talented and creative." Talk to yourself in a positive way, and you will enjoy your life more. You will rise to new levels of confidence and a new level of awareness of your thoughts.

I was in the grocery store the other day in the checkout line. The clerk and a customer were talking and the customer asked "How are you doing today, Peggy?" Peggy replied "Barely making it today. I don't feel well, my husband is getting on my nerves, the kids are going crazy. My life is a mess." The customer said to Peggy "Oh it will get better, just hang in there." Peggy replied "No, it will just get worse." What do you think will likely happen to Peggy? I would bet she will get exactly what she said. You may know someone like Peggy, a coworker maybe. I used to have a coworker named Bill and every morning I would say "Good morning Bill" and Bill would say "What's so good about it?" Bill had a real sour attitude towards life. I decided one day that every morning when Bill would come into work I would say "Good morning Bill." And when he replied "What's so good about it?" I was determined to answer his question. So the next day after I said "Good morning Bill" and Bill said "What's so good about it?", I said to Bill "You are blessed, Bill. That's what's good about it. This morning is a good morning Bill." Bill ignored me and just walked by. This went on for months. Then one day I said "Good morning Bill" and Bill said "good morning

Sylvester." I almost fell over in my chair. Bill said "I am blessed. That's why it is a good morning." I think Bill changed because his self-talk begin to change. He may have seen that his negative thoughts were actually creating his circumstances. In the past his mornings were not good because he didn't see the good in them. When Bill began to see the good in his morning, his self-talk changed from negative to positive.

I am reminded of the optimist creed, which is…

Promise Yourself
To be so strong that nothing can disturb your peace of mind.
To talk health, happiness and prosperity to every person you meet.
To make all your friends feel that there is something in them.
To look at the sunny side of everything and make your optimism come true.
To think only of the best, to work only for the best, and to expect only the best.
To be just as enthusiastic about the success of others as you are about your own.
To forget the mistakes of the past and press on to the greater achievements of the future.
To wear a cheerful countenance at all times and give every living creature you meet a smile.
To give so much time to the improvement of yourself that you have no time to criticize others.

To be too large for worry, too noble for anger, too strong for fear, and too happy to permit the presence of trouble.

The Optimist Creed was first published by Christian D. Larson in 1912

I love that last statement -- to be too large for worry, too noble for anger, too strong to fear, and too happy to permit the presence of trouble. What an awesome statement! I keep a copy of the optimist Creed in my wallet and on my vision board. I think you should keep it close also.

Chapter 7
Health (Your First Wealth)

If we are making a good life better we must live in a healthy body. Our health is our first wealth. Without health we have nothing! Think about it, you can have $100 million in assets and in cash but what good is it to you if you are laying in a hospital bed? What good is the money if your body is always in pain? Health is your first wealth. You must keep your body in the best physical condition as possible. That means eating right, exercise, drinking plenty of water. These are just a few things you need to be conscious of in order to live in a healthy body. One of the basic functions of a healthy life style is exercise. I know some of us do not like to exercise. However, exercise is a must in making a good life better. Here are a few benefits of exercising. Exercise can prevent excess weight gain; when you get enough physical activity you burn calories. You do not have to set aside a large amount of time to exercise. You can do several simple things like taking the stairs instead of the elevator. Maybe parking a little farther away at the grocery store so you can get a nice walk in. Playing with your kids or grandkids. These are just a few things you can do to maintain your weight and at the same time get valuable exercise. Exercise reduces high blood pressure by increasing your HDL cholesterol (the "good cholesterol"), thereby reducing the chance of cardiovascular disease. Exercise improves your mood. If you have had a hard day, going to the gym and working off some steam can really relax you. When you exercise you build your endurance, your physical structure will improve and your confidence will shoot through the roof. Along with exercise we must improve our diets. Diet, of course, also plays an important role in our overall health. In America we love our fast foods. We get up in the morning, we go to a fast food restaurant for breakfast. For lunch we go to a fast food restaurant, and for dinner we go to our favorite fast food restaurant. Fast food is a diet that is high in fat and sodium, something our bodies can do without in excess. Instead of the high-sodium, high-fat diet that fast food places are notorious for, you should choose a diet that is high in fiber, low in fat, and includes lots of antioxidant-enriched foods.

Choosing a diet consisting of fruits, vegetables, whole grains and lean meats will
- reduce risk for stroke and other cardiovascular diseases.
- reduce risk for type 2 diabetes.
- protect against certain cancers, such as stomach, and colon-rectum cancer.
- reduce the risk of coronary artery disease.
- help decrease bone loss and reduce the risk of developing kidney stones.

Fruits and vegetables have no cholesterol and most are naturally low in calories. Vegetables are excellent sources of fiber, potassium, vitamins a, vitamins B and vitamins C.

Let's talk about a few benefits of water.

1. Drinking water helps maintain the balance of body fluids. Your body is composed of about 70% water. The functions of these bodily fluids include digestion, absorption, circulation, creation of saliva, transportation of nutrients, and maintenance of body temperature.
2. Water flushes your kidneys of toxins and other impurities.
3. Your blood is mostly water so drinking the proper amount of water helps to energize your body.

Juicing is a great way to get the nutrients your body needs. It is quick and easy to do. If you are like me I have issues with texture of some fruit and vegetables and find myself avoiding them. However, through juicing I just drink it up with no problem. I juice on a daily basis; I juice kale, spinach, celery, carrots, beets, parsley, and whatever else I feel like juicing.

Go to www.makingagoodlifebetter.com and check out the video I have on my favorite juice. I will show you how to juice properly and also share my favorite maintenance juice. I have a mixture of apple, carrots and ginger. I like the carrots because they are known for their beta carotene which gives the body vitamins A, B, E and many other minerals. Just like the old saying goes, carrots really are good for your eyesight, your bones, teeth, liver, skin, and also may help in preventing some forms of cancer. Apples of course contain antioxidants and also are a good source of fiber. Ginger helps reduce inflammation.

I just want to reiterate that your health is so important. It really is your first wealth. What you eat is also very important; garbage in garbage out as the saying goes. So make sure you put in the proper nutrition in order to feel energized and alert. Get plenty of exercise. If you do not like to exercise get a partner to help motivate you. Drink lots of water. Juice when possible. If you do not have a juicer, there are plenty of inexpensive ones on the market. I recommend you get one as soon as you can. I can't express enough how important juicing can be. These are just a few recommendations that will help maintain that youthful look and energy we all want and deserve. Trust me, your body will love you for it. Now check out the juicing video I have for you at www.makingagoodlifebetter.com

Chapter 8
Loving Relationships

Part of making a good life better is being in loving relationships. It may be in a marriage or a relationship with parents, children or maybe with a best friend. Many people are unhappy and are not experiencing life in its fullest because they close their hearts to loving relationships. If you are blessed enough to be in a loving relationship you need to nurture that relationship. It is very important to your prosperity and your overall wellbeing.

Let's look at the health benefits of a loving relationship between couples.

1. It may boost your immune system. Some research suggests that happy couples have higher functioning immune systems. It seems that you can love your way to health.
2. It can make you physically fit. It turns out that couples who exercise together have more success than people who exercise alone.
3. It might help you live longer. There's a long history of research that has looked at the health benefits of marriage. According to a study by the CDC, mortality rates were found to be the lowest in married couples.

4. It can improve your heart heath. It is found that people in happy relationships experience less stress, which in turn improves their cardiovascular health.

These are just a few health benefits of being in a loving relationship with your spouse.

Communication is a huge part in building and maintaining a loving relationship. Men sometimes fall short in this area. I remember early in my own marriage my wife would come to me with an issue she wanted to discuss about an unpleasant situation at work. She would begin to explain the situation and then I would begin to tell her how she should fix it. As I began to express what I thought she should do, I realize that the only thing she really needed was a listening ear from me. She just needed me to sit and listen not to solve the problem. A word of advice to all the married guys … sometimes you just need to zip it up. Do not give your wife advice on an issue if she does not ask for it. It is very important to keep the lines of communication open. Don't try to guess what each other's needs are; always ask.

Ladies, if you have a husband who is working late or overtime all the time, let him know how much you appreciate what he is doing for the family. Hug him and let him know that he is a great provider for you, and the children if you have children. Assuring words like that really makes a man feel appreciated.

It makes him feel as if he is really providing and taking care of his family. Men always need to be assured that they are appreciated by their wives. Always use encouraging words.

Men, I will let you in on a little secret. You can never say "I love you" enough to your wife. Your wife needs to hear it every day, and several times a day. She needs to know that you are sincere and committed to her and only her. Wives need to feel secure in the marriage, and so do you as a husband. Husbands, let your wie know how much you appreciate the things she does that go unnoticed unless they are not done. Give your wife compliments as often as possible. Let her know how you appreciate how she goes out to work every day just like you. Let your wife know what a great mother she is to your children. You may be blessed enough to have a working wife that takes care of the kids, you and the everyday goings on in the family. That is a wife that should really be appreciated. Give her all the love and kindness she needs.

In a loving relationship like a marriage always build each other up. Never use condemning words to each other. Always build the self-esteem of the other. Criticism does not have a place in a loving relationship. When I say criticism I mean destructive criticism. Destructive criticism of any kind lowers a person's self-esteem faster than any other types of criticism. Destructive criticism has no place in a loving relationship.

In any loving relationship from time to time there will be disagreements. How you handle those disagreements is of the utmost important. Here is an example: Husband, you want to buy a sports car. In your mind you deserve it. You work hard every day; you bring home the bacon, now you want to fry it up. Husband, you tell your wife "Honey I am going to buy a Corvette. I deserve it". Now wife is thinking to herself "What has gotten into you? We have three kids. A corvette is out of the question." However, she says to you very gently and lovingly "Honey you do work hard, you do deserve the Corvette and you will get it. I support you on this a 100%. Right now may not the best time to get your Corvette." Notice how the wife said "your Corvette" giving the husband reassurance that he will indeed get it. Then the wife gives the husband several reasons lovingly as to why it's not the best time to purchase the car, defusing any arguments. Wives have that talent. Believe me, I have been there.

Remember to always build each other up in a loving relationship. The people that are closest to us sometimes feel the most distant because of harsh criticism. In making a good life better we build up and never tear down.

Chapter 9
Stay Positive

In making a good life better it is all about mindset. Maybe you've heard the sayings "what you think about you bring about", "thoughts are things", "energy flows were attention goes". All these statements are true statements. So in making a good life better you want to stay positive. You want to speak of only what you want. Remember to keep any thoughts that are not in line with what you desire out of your mind. All thoughts that are not on the same track as your intentions and your desires should be discarded immediately.

Remember, thoughts really are things so keep your thoughts on your desires. So often I hear people say "I don't want this" or "I don't want that". Instead of saying what you don't want, speak of only what you do want. Let's say you are asked by your spouse to attend a function at the in-laws' home, and in the past those types of events have not gone so well. It is really important to your spouse that you attend. In your mind picture the entire visit. Visualize how you want the visit to go. As you learned in the chapter on visualization, this is a powerful technique that works. It will be a pleasant visit just as you visualized it to be.

Another thing you should keep in mind is that it is always good to speak well of others. We always get what we put out in either words or actions. If you give out pleasant thoughts you will receive and produce pleasant thoughts. Wish for others what you wish for yourself. Speak of peace, health and prosperity toward other people. As you shop at the grocery store mentally speak abundance to the people around you. As you walk aisle by aisle speak health to the people around you. (Not out loud; they may think you have a problem!) Silently to yourself, wish everyone you pass health and prosperity. Wishing them health and prosperity will bring health and prosperity to you.

Speak well of your coworkers. I know this can be difficult sometimes; however, speak mentally of them what you want for yourself. Leave the water cooler gossip to the gossips. I have heard it said that "your light will not shine brighter by trying to put someone else's light out."

Not only should you speak well of others; you should also speak well of yourself. If you are married say to yourself "I am a great spouse" even if you know that you can improve in some areas. This will help you to make those improvements.

Do not be concerned about what people will think because you speak well of yourself. I have been around people who when making a mistake would call themselves dummy out loud. Or they would say "I am so stupid" or "what a moron I am." Believe me, you do not want to speak those kinds of things over your life. Remember we get what we put out. Thoughts are really things that become manifested into our lives. What would be better to say in a case like that is to say "wow I am better than that; next time I will get it right. Use the power of saying "I Am." "I am" are two of the most powerful words that you can use. The bible says that "death and life are in the power of the tongue and those who love it will eat its fruit" You want to produce good fruits by speaking good after your "I am". Whatever you say after "I am", you will likely become. Say things like "I am a patient person", "I am an understanding parent", "I am a great neighbor", "I am a great contributor to my company", "I am a multimillionaire", "I am a child of the most high God". What an awesome feeling you will have just speaking these things to yourself. Use your "I am" wisely. Be bold; declare the "I AM" with confidence and expectancy. Know that you are "I AM" and will get whatever you declare after you speak "I AM". So use it wisely; don't mess it up!

Remember to go to www.makingagoodlifebetter.com and check out the four bonuses I have for you.

Chapter 10
Put your New Power to Work!

You may think right now that what you want is still a long way off, but actually it is closer than you think. You are making a good life better by developing a lifestyle through some of the suggestions in this book. You are beginning to realize that the things you think about you bring about. You are realizing that if you continue to move forward you will achieve sooner than you think. Just keep in mind what you really want for your life. The things that we have been talking about throughout this book. Keep, in the forefront of your mind, believing in yourself. Believing that you can achieve the things you want. Continue to keep what you want in the forefront of your mind. Remember to live as if you already have the money that you desire, you already have the health that you desire, you already have the prosperity, you already have the success that you desire. Just walk and talk as if you already have what you want because in fact you really do. You are equipped with the tools and the knowledge to become the person that you want to be. As you know by now it all starts with the way we think.

Let's briefly review the 10 steps in making a good life better.

In chapter one we talked about desire. We found that Webster defines desire as is a strong feeling of wanting something. To crave, to want, to long for something. You learned that you need to know what you want and have a clear picture of it in your mind.

In chapter two we talked about visualization. The dictionary defines visualization as the formation of mental visual images or pictures. Images and pictures that are actually seen in the eyes of the mind. We must first see it in the eyes of our mind before we can bring it into our reality.

In chapter three we learned the power of affirmations. Affirmations are defined as an act of affirming: to declare positively something to be true. "Calleth those things which be not as though they were." You wrote your own affirmation and committed it memory. Whatever it is will began to show up in your life.

In chapter four we learned to be grateful. Being grateful is one of the most powerful conditions you can allow yourself to be in. Being grateful for what you have now will bring even more things into your life to be grateful for. Staying in gratitude has a boomerang effect; more things to be grateful for will come back to you.

In chapter five we learned to bring prosperity into our life. Prosperity is the state of flourishing, thriving, having good fortune and or successful social status. We all want to thrive and flourish not only for ourselves but also for our loved ones. Think and speak only of prosperity into your life. Remember we are" Making A Good Life Better."

In chapter six we learned the importance of self-talk. We are in conversation with ourselves every minute of every day. We talk more to ourselves than to anyone else. So keep the conversations that you have with yourself uplifting, positive and hopeful about your future, because it is very bright!

Chapter seven is one of my favorites. We learned the importance of health. If you have not yet checked out my video on the importance of juicing, go to www.makingagoodlifebetter.com and look at the video I have on my favorite juicing recipe. As I stated, health is our first wealth.

In chapter eight we learned the importance of loving relationships. We learned the important health benefits being in a loving relationship can bring. People in loving relationships actually do live longer than people who are not in a loving relationship.

In chapter nine we learned to stay positive. We learned that what we think about we bring about. We learned that thoughts are things. So you want to keep your mind and your thoughts on the positive things in your life.

So you are now equipped with all the tools you need in Making A Good Life Better. Put everything you have learned together and you will without fail make all your dreams come true.

I will see you at the top!

Be sure to go to www.makingagoodlifebetter.com and get your Making A Good Life Better T-shirt.

NOTES

NOTES

NOTES

NOTES

NOTES

NOTES